A New True Book

ELK

By Emilie U. Lepthien

CHILDRENS PRESS®

CHICAGO

A mother elk with
her newborn calf

PHOTO CREDITS

© Reinhard Brucker–4; Field Museum, Chicago, 31
(2 photos), 33 (right); Ft. Laramie, Wyoming, 33 (left)

Jerry Hennen–15

© Bill Ivy–11

© Emilie Lepthien–© Seattle Filmworks, 14

Root Resources–© Diana Stratton, 2; © Mary A. Root,
45

Tom Stack & Associates–© Greg Vaughn, 8; © Diana
L. Stratton, 27 (right); © Barbara von Hoffmann, 35

Tony Stone Images–© Timothy Lucas, 36; © Tom
Ulrich, 39

SuperStock International, Inc.–© A. Mercieca, 7;
© M. Carlisle, 10

Valan–© Albert Kuhnigk, Cover, 16, 19 (right); © Bob
Gurr, 5 (left); © Murray O'Neill, 5 (right); © Hälle
Flygare, 9, 29; © Aubrey Lang, 13, 24, 45; © Esther
Schmidt, 19 (left); © Jean Sloman, 20; © Jeff Foott, 21;
© Wayne Lankinen, 41 (left); © James D. Markou, 41
(right)

Visuals Unlimited–© Les Christman, 17, 40; © Len
Rue, Jr., 23; © Michael S. Quinton, 26, 27 (left); © Joe
McDonald, 43

COVER: Male Elk (Wapiti)

Project Editor: Fran Dyra
Design: Margrit Fiddle

Library of Congress Cataloging-in-Publication Data

Lepthien, Emilie U. (Emilie Utteg)
    Elk / by Emilie U. Lepthien.
        p.   cm.–(A New true book)
    Includes index.
    ISBN 0-516-01063-8
    1.   Elk–Juvenile literature. [1. Elk.] I. Title.
QL737.U55L45   1994
599.73'57–dc20   94-10469
                              CIP
                              AC

TABLE OF CONTENTS

The name *wapiti* means "white rump" in the Shawnee language.

ELK OR *WAPITI*

The Shawnee people called them *wapiti,* meaning "white rump." The European settlers who landed in North America over 350 years ago called them "elk."

Elk belong to the deer family, or Cervidae. They are relatives of the moose, white-tailed deer, caribou, and reindeer.

Caribou (left) and white-tailed deer (below) are relatives of the elk.

These animals are found in Europe, Asia, and North America. In North America, they are sometimes called *wapiti*. But more often they are known as American elk. The European elk is *Alces alces*. It is the animal we know as the moose.

Like other members of the deer family, elk are ungulates—they have hooves. They are also mammals. Their young feed on mother's milk.

The elk's keen senses of hearing and smell help protect the animal from predators.

end of its 5-inch (13-centimeter) tail. Females, or cows, are smaller.

Elk have keen senses of smell and hearing. Their sharp ears and nose warn them if a predator is near.

11

Their legs are long and strong. Elk can run at speeds of up to 30 miles (48 kilometers) per hour and leap over high fences.

Elk are brownish gray with a lighter, yellowish patch on the rump. Their legs, head, and neck are dark brown. In the fall, elk grow a thick undercoat that keeps them warm in winter. In spring, the animals molt, or shed their winter fur. Their summer coat is thin and smooth.

An elk uses the hard pad of flesh on its upper gum to hold food while the bottom teeth tear the food off the plant.

SPECIAL TEETH AND HOOVES

Elk have thirty-four teeth. There are six sharp incisors in the front of the lower jaw, but elk have no front teeth in the upper jaw. Instead, there is a hard pad of flesh on the upper

13

gum. They use this pad and their lower incisors to tear off leaves and twigs.

Both male and female elk have two large teeth called elk tusks in their upper jaw. In the past, many elk were killed for these tusks.

Like all members of the deer family, elk have split hooves. Their hard split hooves help the animals walk on rough ground.

An elk's hoof is divided into two parts. This is called a cloven hoof.

CHEWING THE CUD

In summer, elk mainly eat grasses. In winter, they often eat the twigs and needles of trees and shrubs.

Elk have four separate stomach pouches. They swallow their food quickly without chewing. The food is collected in the first

An elk in winter, eating the needles of a pine tree

Elk chew their cud with a side-to-side motion of the jaw.

pouch. Then it passes into the second pouch, where it is softened and formed into balls called cuds.

The cuds are spit up to be chewed until they are a fine pulp. Then the cuds are swallowed and the food is digested in the third and fourth stomach pouches.

ANTLERS

Bull elk shed their antlers in late winter each year. Soon new antlers begin to grow. In four months they are fully grown and hardened into strong bone. Cows have no antlers.

An arch made of elk antlers that were shed by the animals

The antlers may weigh from 40 to 50 pounds (18 to 23 kilograms) and measure 5 feet (1.5 meters) across.

An elk's first antlers appear when the animal is ten to eleven months old. A one-year-old elk's antlers are just spikes 10 to 20 inches (25 to 51 centimeters) long. A four-year-old elk has six or seven tines—or points—on each antler. The antlers

The antlers of a one-year-old bull elk (above) are small spikes. A three-year-old bull (right) has larger antlers with several branches.

get bigger each year until the bulls are seven or eight years old.

While they are growing, antlers are covered with a soft layer of skin called velvet. Blood vessels in

19

The growing antlers are covered with soft, fuzzy velvet.

the velvet carry nutrients
to the growing antlers.

By July or early August,
the antlers have stopped
growing. The bulls rub their
antlers against trees or
bushes to remove the velvet.

A bull elk gathers his harem in a clearing, where he can watch the cows.

season, he gathers a
harem—a group of six to
thirty or more cows.

If another bull tries to
take a cow from the

23

Bull elk shove each other with their antlers.
The stronger bull will win the match.

harem, the herd bull displays his huge antlers. Usually this is enough to make the other bull go away. But if a bull with very large antlers challenges the herd bull, there will be a fight.

Using their antlers, the bulls shove each other. Finally, the stronger bull is the winner. Usually the challenger runs away.

After the mating season, the bulls leave the cows and form small herds of males. The bulls eat little during the mating season. Now they must make up for lost time.

In winter, elk often dig through 12 inches (30

In winter, bulls gather in small groups.

centimeters) of snow with their hooves and noses to find food. In deeper snow, they may be unable to find grasses, twigs, or berries. Many suffer from hunger.

26

An elk calf can stand soon after birth (left). Mother elk stay near the calves to protect them from predators.

CALVES

In spring, the cows go off by themselves to feed on the new shoots of grass. Calves are born in late May. Their average weight at birth is 30 pounds (13 kilograms).

Their coat is reddish brown with many white spots. Calves can stand shortly after birth. The next day, they try to run.

An elk calf is hunted by cougars, bears, wolves, coyotes, and even golden eagles.

Luckily, its spotted coat makes it hard for predators to see. And when the mother leaves her calf to feed, the calf stays very still. The mother

A herd of elk cows and calves crossing the Kicking Horse River in Yoho National Park, Canada

runs to protect her calf if a predator comes near.

When the calves are about one week old, mothers and calves join a herd of females, yearlings, and calves. Two or three

29

mothers watch the calves while the other cows go off to eat.

Calves begin to nurse as soon as they can stand. After only a few weeks, they can eat grass. But they still need their mother's milk until late fall. By then they are usually weaned.

Calves communicate by squealing. Cows use a high-pitched sound to call the calf to nurse.

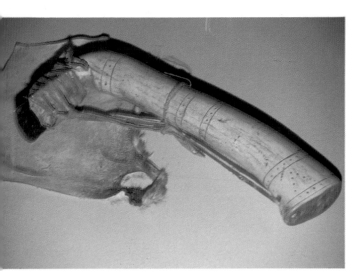

A Native American hide scraper made of elk antler
and a dress decorated with elk's teeth

VALUABLE ANIMALS

The Native Americans used
every part of the elk. The
animal provided meat for
food and hides for clothing.
The bones were used to
make tools and utensils.

European settlers used
elk fat to make candles.

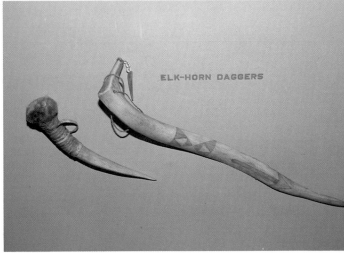

An elk-hide shirt and
elk-antler daggers used
by Native Americans

Antlers were made into
furniture, handles for knives,
and glue. Clothing and
footwear were made from
elk hides. But the 400
pounds (181 kilograms) of
meat each animal supplied
was most important.

ELK TODAY

Before North America was settled by Europeans, elk roamed across what is now the United States and north into Canada. In the year 1760, there may have been 10 million elk on the North American continent.

After farms were established, people wanted to get rid of the elk herds. Farmers thought the elk were taking feed from their cattle. They did not realize that one dairy cow ate as much grass daily as three elk. As a result, the elk were slaughtered. By 1919 there were only about 70,000 left in the United States.

Today, there are almost 400,000 elk in the United States and 46,000 in Canada.

Montana, Idaho, Colorado, Oregon, and Washington each have over 50,000 elk. Wyoming

Elk herd grazing in Rocky Mountain National Park

has over 70,000. There are
11,000 in New Mexico and
over 5,000 in Utah. In
some places, such as
Yellowstone and Grand
Teton national parks, there
are more elk than the land
can support.

35

Elk spending the winter in the National Elk Refuge in Wyoming

ELK REFUGES

When winter is coming, many elk travel as far as 100 miles (161 kilometers) to reach the National Elk Refuge in Jackson Hole,

Wyoming. On the way, they avoid areas where there are hunters. In Oklahoma, elk spend the winter in the Wichita Mountains Wildlife Refuge.

Other wildlife refuges supply the elk with hay to supplement their diet. In the United States, most elk spend the summer in Yellowstone, Grand Teton,

Glacier, Olympic, and Rocky Mountain national parks.

Roosevelt elk were brought to Afognak Island, Alaska, in the 1920s. Today, that herd numbers about 1,000.

British Columbia in Canada has about 30,000 elk. These animals spend the summer in Banff and Jasper national parks.

In winter, the mountain snows are deep, and elk

cannot find food. They
must migrate to lower
regions where food is
more plentiful.

The National Elk Refuge has grassy meadows for good grazing.

Without the National Elk Refuge, and other wildlife refuges and preserves, many elk would starve to death each winter.

CONTROLLING POPULATION

At one time, the elk's chief predator was the wolf. Smaller predators—the fisher, lynx, fox, and wolverine—depended on the wolf to share elk carcasses. But, over time,

The red fox (left) and the fisher (below) shared elk carcasses with the wolves.

so many wolves were
killed that they became an
endangered species. There
were no wolves left in
Yellowstone, Grand Teton,
or Glacier national parks.

Without the wolves' leftovers,
the smaller predators also
declined in number. The elk
population increased by 20
percent a year.

Overpopulation of elk
grazing lands became a
problem.

In 1994 the United
States Fish and Wildlife

Wolves feeding on an elk carcass. These predators play an important role in keeping the elk population under control.

Service reintroduced wolves into Yellowstone National Park. These wolves may help maintain the balance of nature by preying on elk, deer, and other animals.

Elk cows in Yellowstone National Park. We must preserve the natural environment of wild places if the elk is to survive.

Hunters are used to control the elk population. Each year hunters with special licenses shoot several hundred elk.

We must protect the four

remaining subspecies of American elk from extinction. Ways must be found to restore the balance of nature between the magnificent American elk and its environment.

WORDS YOU SHOULD KNOW

Alces alces (AL • sez AL • sez)–the European elk; the American moose

antlers (ANT • lerz)–bony, hornlike growths on the head of an animal such as a deer or a moose

blood vessels (BLUHD VESS • ilz)–tubes that carry blood through the body

Cervidae (SER • vih • day)–the deer family

challenge (CHAL • enje)–to dare one to take part in a fight or contest

decline (dih • KLYNE)–to gradually become fewer in number

endangered (en • DAIN • jerd)–in danger of dying out

environment (en • VYE • ron • mint)–the things that surround a plant or an animal; the lands and waters of the earth

extinction (ex • TINK • shun)–the dying out of a plant or animal species

harem (HAIR • um)–a group of cows that a bull elk gathers to mate with

hide (HYDE)–the skin of an animal

incisors (in • SYE • zerz)–long, sharp front teeth

license (LY • sense)–a permit to do something, such as hunt animals or drive a car

mammal (MAM • il)– one of a group of warm-blooded animals that have hair and nurse their young with milk

migrate (MY • grait)–to travel, usually for a long distance, to find better food or better weather conditions

molt (MOHLT)–to shed hair, especially a thick winter coat

moose (MOOSE)–a very large deer with broad antlers

nutrients (NOO • tree • ints)–elements that are essential to keep living things strong and healthy, such as proteins, carbohydrates, fats, vitamins, and minerals

plentiful (PLEN • tih • ful)–in good supply; abundant

population (pop • yoo • LAY • shun)–the total number of animals of the same kind living at the same time

predator (PREH • di • ter)–an animal that kills and eats other animals

refuge (REH • fyooj)–a place where an animal can be safe from its enemies

subspecies (SUHB • spee • seez)–groups of related animals that all belong to the same species but are slightly different

tines (TYNES)–points; blades

ungulates (UNG • gyoo • lates)–animals with hooves

utensils (yoo • TEN • silz)–objects used in everyday life, such as knives, pots, and spoons

wapiti (wah • PEE • tee)–the Shawnee name for the American elk

weaned (WEEND)–starting to eat solid food instead of mother's milk

INDEX

About the Author

Emilie U. Lepthien received her BA and MS degrees and certificate in school administration from Northwestern University. She taught upper-grade science and social studies, wrote and narrated science programs for the Chicago Public Schools' station WBEZ, and was principal in Chicago, Illinois, for twenty years. She received the American Educator's Medal from Freedoms Foundation.

She is a member of Delta Kappa Gamma Society International, Chicago Principals' Association, Illinois Women's Press Association, National Federation of Press Women, and AAUW.

She has written books in the Enchantment of the World, New True Books, and America the Beautiful series.